GUINEA PIGS

Hans L. Schippers

GUINEA PIGS

REBO
PUBLISHERS

© 1998 Zuid Boekprodukties
© 2006 Rebo Publishers

Text: Hans L. Schippers
Photographs: The Goedhart family, Rob Doolaard, and Hans L. Schippers
Cover design: Minkowsky Graphic Design, Enkhuizen, The Netherlands
Typesetting and pre-press services: A. R. Garamond, Prague, The Czech Republic
Translation: Stephen Challacombe
Proofreading: Sarah Dunham

ISBN 13: 978-90-366-1560-0
ISBN 10: 90-366-1560-7

Contents

INTRODUCTION

The guinea pig or cavy is undoubtedly one of the most popular of pets because it is ideal for both young and old and can be handled and stroked. They are mostly well-behaved animals that rarely bite and are easily cared for by children. What is more, guinea pigs do not take up much space and so they are suitable for those living in smaller homes. A cavy need not be expensive. Later in this book there is advice about the things you must pay attention to when buying or acquiring a guinea pig. There is a wide range of different options for accommodation available: first class and spacious cages for those who want to keep guinea pigs indoors, fine wooden hutches for outside, and complete racks of cages for professional breeders. Feeding guinea pigs requires special attention. Some feeds are not as good as others. The current thinking on guinea pig

Golden Satin with several day old offspring

nutrition is thoroughly dealt with the tremendous importance of vitamin C to guinea pigs. With the rapid growth in different varieties of guinea pigs in recent years, there is a need for factual information about the different breeds and varieties, and this too is extensively covered. The book of course deals with the older traditional types as well as the newer varieties. There is also information about guinea pig behavior, handling and how to relate to them, breeding, and the prevention of and treatment of illnesses. This book provides the information that both newcomers and experienced breeders alike need in order to keep guinea pigs in a responsible and caring way.

Right:
Red Dutch

1 THE HISTORY OF THE GUINEA PIG OR CAVY

Cavies, or guinea pigs as they have been popularly known, originate from Peru and Chile in South America, where they can still be found in the wild. When they were discovered in South America, guinea pigs were being kept by the Incas in Peru, both as pets and sacrificial animals. At that time, there were variations in color such as red, brown, black, and bicolored animals. The animals provided a welcome change to the daily diet and continue to be eaten in various countries of South America. A number of types of cavy live in the wild,

Several attractive modern varieties

where they remain together in family groups. Our pet guinea pigs originate from the wild cavy, *Cavia aperaea porcellus*, which is similarly colored to the natural or wild Golden agouti with its warmish red coat with regular black "ticking." This is the original color for guinea pigs.

Guinea pigs were brought to Europe toward the end of the sixteenth century by way of the west or Guinea coast of Africa, although they must already have been known in Europe before this— the Swiss biologist Conrad Gessner described them in his Tierenbuch (Book of animals) in 1553. He was the founder of the University of Zürich botanical garden. His description and illustrations more or less match the present-day cavy. Like the Spanish, he called them "Indian rabbits." He wrote convincingly of how these animals had been discovered by explorers in the recently discovered "New World" and brought back to England via Spain and Portugal, what the ani-

Right: Engraving in copper by Jacques DeSeve from about 1750 of a three-colored cavy. Guinea pigs were clearly much longer then.

Golden agouti

mals ate, the colors that were known in his days, and how guinea pigs reproduced. It was not until the end of the nineteenth century, however, that the guinea pig became well known as a household pet. England played a major role in this process.

Guinea pigs did not really becamebecome widely popular until after World War II, although unfortunately they had become increasingly widely used as laboratory animals. This resulted, however, in greater scientific knowledge and led to the development of better feeds for the animals.

Today, they are widely kept as pets and virtually every country has a national organization for guinea pigs, reflecting this widespread interest. In everyday language, the term "guinea pig" continues in popular use, as a result of historical misconception concerning their origin. Because newcomers to these animals will generally know them as "guinea pigs," this term has been used together with cavy in this book. Male guinea pigs are termed "boars," while females are "sows," just like pigs. The French call them *cochon d'Inde* or "Indian pig."

A spacious cage provides room for several guinea pigs.

Dutch red

2 GETTING A GUINEA PIG

Before you get a guinea pig it is best to ask yourself for which purpose you want to keep it and which one will be best suited to your needs. Do you want to breed a special type and enter it in shows? Would you prefer a calm, easily handled breed, or rather have an active and lively guinea pig? Do you want a normal-haired guinea pig or one of the long-hairedlonghaired varieties? Do you have plenty of spare time to care for the animal or very little? It is best to think about these matters before you buy or acquire your guinea pig. Obtain as much informa-

Guinea pigs make ideal children's pets because they are easily handled.

Right: cream guinea pig with offspring

tion as you can about keeping guinea pigs. You may be able to get help and advice from a local club for guinea pig fanciers. The better pet shops are also able to give you information

about looking after guinea pigs. It is not advisable to buy a guinea pig at a market because it is too difficult under these circumstances to check the condition of the animal. Sometimes the animals may be weak from having traveled a long way, making them susceptible to illness. Specimens can sometimes be bought at guinea pig shows. It is certainly a good idea to read several books on the subject and to have some for future reference too. The more you know about guinea pigs, the smaller the risk of your purchase being a great disappointment.

Guinea pigs are ideal pets for children, as indicated earlier, because they are easily handled. Adults too, however, can get a great deal of pleasure from keeping guinea pigs, provided the right choice is made. Pay careful attention when getting a guinea pig to the following points:

- The animal's age: an ideal age is not less than five weeks old. Many guinea pigs are sold when too young and suffer as a result.
- The health and general condition: the guinea pig should appear lively and interested.
- The sturdiness: a guinea pig should feel sturdy to the

Make sure when buying a guinea pig that it seems lively and alert.

Guinea pigs gathered around a hay manger

touch when held. It is best to avoid rather thin and weedy specimens.

- The hair (of the normal-haired types) should be shiny, sleek, and without bald patches or loose hairs.
- The nose, eyes, and ears should be clean.
- The teeth should appear normal.
- Droppings should be elongated and dry. The droppings should not be at all runny and none should have clung to the hairs surrounding the anus.

Ask the previous owner of the guinea pig what feed it was given and give the animal the same. If the feeding regime needs to be changed because of problems such as diarrhea, make sure the change is introduced gradually.

The price of an ordinary guinea pig depends upon its age and quality. Peruvian and Abyssinian guinea pigs are more expensive, and unusual breeds such as Texel, Rex, or Silkies are among the most expensive.

3 ACCOMMODATION

In the wild, guinea pigs live in family groups and large colonies and therefore they are fairly tolerant. A group of guinea pigs will have a specific hierarchy, yet they can be kept as single animals provided they are used to this from a young age. Your guinea pig's welfare demands that you give it some attention each day, and that it is not shut away without contact with the outside world. If this is not the case, the guinea pig will slowly pine away. If your guinea pig appears to be lonely, give it a companion of the same sex. Guinea pigs make a very close bond with the person who cares for them daily and they are creatures of habit, quickly adopting set patterns in their life and care. The accommodation needs to be suitable, both for the guinea pig(s) and your circumstances and plans. There is a great difference between keeping one guinea pig for company and setting up to breed them.

A guinea pig "village," complete with church

All manner of cages and hutches can be found in specialist shops, but not all of them are suitable for the purpose. Avoid the smaller cages. Guinea pigs can be kept out of doors in both summer and winter provided they have sufficient shelter, but they must then be given additional hay in their cage. If there is a long period of frosty weather, it is best to move the cage into a shed.

Right: a fine family home for a guinea pig

An indoor cage

Guinea pigs originally lived out of doors in the wild, so if they are kept in a cage indoors, it needs to be spacious, especially if you wish to keep several guinea pigs. Most indoor cages have a plastic tray at the bottom, with a removable upper section with metal bars. Such a cage should be about 24 x 16 in. (60 x 40 cm) and about 16 in. (40 cm) high. A smooth-bottomed cage can be made non-slip by putting in a piece of waterproof hardboard, rough side up. Most enthusiasts choose vertical bars for their cages because guinea pigs can easily get their feet or teeth stuck in horizontal bars, which can cause injuries.

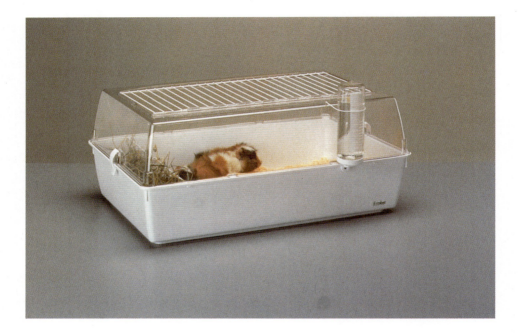

Modern plastic indoor cage, with virtually draft-free upper section

Where you place the cage is also important. The position should neither be too warm nor too damp, and there must not be a drauftdraft. Consequently, near a window in the full sun, next to a radiator, or close to a door that is constantly being opened and closed is entirely the wrong place. Other pets, such as cats and dogs, should not pose any problems since they should quickly become accustomed to each other. Of course, you must make sure that they cannot actually reach the guinea pig. An indoor cage needs to be able to be closed properly. The best bedding for the cage is a layer of white sawdust about 1½ in. (3 cm) thick, covered with sufficient hay for the guinea pig to be able to hide in. A heavy feeding trough of earthenware is far better than a lightweight plastic one, which is likely to get pushed all around the cage. A drinking bottle is far better than a bowl, which is likely to become dirty rather quickly. The drinking water must be changed every day. If the inside of the bottle becomes dirty, place a handful of uncooked rice in the bottle and shake it well. Rinse the bottle before refilling it. Green feed is best given in a special container that fastens to the side of the cage, where the food is less likely to become soiled.

Indoor cages for guinea pigs are generally cleaned out so frequently that they never smell, but in practice twice per week is sufficient. If there are more guinea pigs in the cage, it will obviously need cleaning out more often. Because guinea pigs have no natural play instincts, there is no need to provide them with toys. It is a good idea, however, to keep them regularly supplied with fresh willow or fruit tree branches to gnaw on.

Indoor cage with upper section of metal bars. The cage is an ideal shape and size, with a bottom tray that is deep enough.

A guinea pig hutch

An outdoor hutch for guinea pigs has to fulfill a number of requirements. It needs to be larger than an indoor cage because, when the weather is cold, it will need to be filled with lots of hay to keep the guinea pigs warm. Choose a hutch rather than an outside run, as experience has shown that guinea pigs are not able to cope with being without shelter in a northern climate. An outside run is not a problem on a warm, sunny day. Some breeds have special needs in terms of their accommodation. The Peruvian varieties have to be housed in such a way that the risk of their hair becoming dirty is minimized. They are best kept on a layer of sawdust with a very thin layer of hay.

An outside hutch needs to be at least 27 x 19 in. (70 x 50 cm) with a height of at least 17 in. (45 cm). A larger hutch is preferable for Peruvian guinea pigs, or if you intend keeping more animals in the same hutch, or if you will need to keep a guinea pig with its offspring. It is quite easy to make a suitable hutch for a guinea pig yourself. The best material is marine ply, which is suitably smooth, requires no seams or joints, and is therefore easy to keep clean. Lay a piece of waterproof hardboard with the rough side uppermost on the floor of the cage, because ply is too smooth for guinea pigs to walk on. Cover this with a layer of sawdust and place a layer of hay on top of this. Straw is not really suitable for guinea pigs, because it is too coarse and hard and can lead to them injuring their eyes. It is best to have two doors in the front of the hutch, because guinea pigs can escape too easily from hutches with single doors. Fasten bars, or better still, mink netting $^3/_4$ x $^3/_4$ in. (19 x 19 mm), to the doors. It is better to fasten the feeding tray to the side of the hutch rather than the front, where it might block the view. Use a heavy feeding trough big enough for the number of guinea pigs you intend to keep. Complete the hutch with a drinking bottle fastened at a suitable height.

A guinea pig run

A run can make a suitable temporary home for guinea pigs during the spring and summer months. It is fairly easy to make a run yourself. The length should not be less than 5 ft. (152 cm), including the night accommodation, and should be about 20 in. (50 cm) high. Do not make the run too small, particularly if you want to breed young ones, for they grow rapidly but the run remains the same size. For the same reason, the night accommodation needs to be sufficiently spacious. Make sure the bottom of the run is covered with fine netting, to prevent young guinea pigs from escaping and to keep out intruders. Such a run can be placed on a lawn. By moving the run each day, you maintain hygienic conditions and also provide the guinea pigs with fresh grass.

An outdoor run is a suitable home for guinea pigs in the spring and summer.

An apartment block

Those who really become involved in breeding guinea pigs often need plenty of space. To keep many guinea pigs in a small area, the solution can be a bank of cages rather like a guinea pig apartment block. These have proved to be entirely satisfactory. Such a bank of cages can be made from _ in. (12 mm) marine ply. The six cage unit illustrated is 48 in. (120 cm) wide, 32 in. (80 cm) high, and 24 in. (61 cm) deep. The individual hutches are 16 in. (40 cm) wide and high, and 24 in. (61 cm) deep. Each cage has its own door, with removable trays for the bottom litter to prevent it falling out when the door is opened. If the partition walls are also made to be removable, the cage can be adapted for small and large guinea pigs. The timber is glued, screwed, and nailed to prevent there being any joints, in the interests of hygiene. The hinges, catches, and netting have to be stainless steel or galvanized. Treat the floor of each hutch with waterproof bituminous paint to give it longer life. The entire structure can be painted or, better still, varnished. The number of individual hutches in a set of cages like this can easily be adapted to your wishes. It is also possible to buy such units ready-made for a reasonable price.

Remember that guinea pigs needs liquid, whether from their green fodder or drinking water. The greater the amount of fresh green feed that is available to them, the less will be the demand for water. If your guinea pig gets plenty of green matter, it will also urinate more. In this case, place a thicker layer of sawdust on the bottom of the cage to absorb the additional moisture. The cage will, of course, also need cleaning more frequently.

Young, tricolor Peruvian guinea pig

4 FEEDING

Guinea pigs are herbivores; in other words, they eat plants. The digestive system works rather slowly and food takes between two and seven days to be digested. Feeding is an important part of the overall care of guinea pigs, because they have some specific needs in their nutrition. The requirement of vitamin C is one remarkable feature, as they are unable to produce it themselves. Hence it is advisable to use specially-developed vitamin C feeds. Rodent and rabbit food is only acceptable if the levels of protein and vitamin C, which are generally too low, are supplemented. This can be done by giving large amounts of green fodder and fruit. In reality, rodent and rabbit food can only be regarded as part of a guinea pig's diet. Because in the wild, guinea pigs eat several times each day, it is best to feed them twice daily.

Peppers and carrots are full of vitamin C and guinea pigs love them.

Right: a varied diet helps the young to grow rapidly and be healthy.

A good basic diet for guinea pigs consists of:
- A handful of fresh hay each day. Guinea pigs must not be without this because it is essential to their digestion.
- About 1–1.5 oz (30–40 g) complete guinea pig feed per day.
- Fresh grass or green fodder.
- Fresh water daily.
- For variety: stale bread, carrot, segments of orange, apple, or pear, cucumber, sugar beet, mangelred beet, and wild herbs. Peppers are ideal food because they are rich in vitamin C and guinea pigs adore them.

Important things to know about nutrition

Food provides the energy necessary for important living functions such as the circulation of the blood, digestion, and intestinal movement. Heat is produced from the consumption of energy.

Nutrition is also important to keep the body healthy. Certain nutritional elements are essential for growth and for reproduction. A balanced diet includes both dry matter and moisture. Dry matter can be divided into organic (combustible) and inorganic (non-combustible) matter. Carbohydrates, proteins, and fats are organic, but minerals and salts are inorganic matter.

If the droppings of your guinea pig appear like this, then it is healthy.

Water

A drinking bottle is better than a bowl, which soils quickly.

Water forms an important part of the diet. It functions as:
- Body matter: much of a guinea pig's body consists of water.
- Solvent: before the nutritional elements of a food can pass into the bloodstream, they first have to dissolve in water.
- Transport: food is transported to the smallest parts of the body by the blood, which substantially consists of water.
- Protection for the mucous membranes.
- Thermostat: the body temperature of a guinea pig is in the range 99.5–102.2°F (37.5–39°C).

Hay is essential for the digestion.

Carbohydrates

Carbohydrates are organic compounds made up of carbon, oxygen, and hydrogen. Carbohydrates consist of starch, sugars, glycogen, and cellulose or fiber. Fiber is essential to the digestive process. This is why it is absolutely vital that guinea pigs eat hay each day.

Carbohydrates are the principal sources of energy in food. A surplus of carbohydrate can be converted into fat. The major source of carbohydrate is starch, which is found in various types of grain. A good guinea pig food contains about thirteen percent carbohydrate.

Protein

Protein is essential in the creation of tissue and organs, and consists of amino acids of which some 20 are known. Guinea pig food should contain about 12 of these amino acids, with lysine, leucine, methionine, and valine being the most important for guinea pigs.

Amino acids are the basic constituents of proteins and they are found in both animals and vegetables. Guinea pig food comprises about twenty percent raw protein. Proteins can also be partially converted into fat to provide a reserve for days when there is not enough to eat.

Fat

Fat is also a source of energy, providing about two-and-a-half times as much energy as the same amount of carbohydrate. Small amounts of fat in a feed are healthy for a guinea pig, resulting in the animal achieving its nutritional needs with less food, growing more quickly, and developing a shiny coat. Tests have shown that guinea pigs prefer a feed containing about four and a half percent fat. This is because the fat contains smells and tastes that make the food more appealing. Body fat can store vitamins A, D, E, and K.

Vitamins

Vitamins are organic compounds that are essential to the body's metabolism. A deficiency of vitamins can lead to serious nutritional disorders and illness. To prevent this, the diet must be balanced, varied, and rich in vitamins. If food is heated or stored for a long time, the vitamin content can be reduced, lost entirely, or its efficacy can be affected. Food that is known to be rich in vitamins includes green-leafed fodder,

Various feeding bowls. The left-hand bowl is the best—it cannot tip over and has a removable stainless steel inner bowl. The center bowls are suitable for use as drinking bowls. The right-hand bowl is too light and can be easily overturned.

fruit, especially lemon, milk, and cod-liver oil. A description of the different vitamins and their working follows.

Vitamin A

Vitamin A (axerophtol) is found in green plants, fruit, and animal products. Kale, Brussels sprouts, grass, clover, carrots, hay or silage, and maize are all rich in vitamin A. Vitamin A also occurs in the form of carotene, a vitamin precursor. Vitamin A is important for the health of the skin, the mucous membranes, windpipe, intestinal linings, eye sockets, and fallopian tubes. This vitamin is also very important in reproduction and growth, and helps to strengthen the immune system. A deficiency in vitamin A slows down growth, and makes a guinea pig more susceptible to eye complaints, throat infections, skin ailments, and

inflammations. Guinea pig food should contain about 9,000 international units (IU) per pound (20,000 per kg) of vitamin A.

Feeding time for the babies

Vitamin B

Vitamin B is a complex of vitamins such as B1, B2, B6, and B12. They are found in green fodder, legumes (peas and beans), and milk products, but are also formed by bacteria in the gut. The following B vitamins are important for guinea pigs.

Vitamin B1 (thiamine) is necessary for the absorption of energy foods and to stimulate the appetite. It also helps to prevent nervous system disorders. A guinea pig will get sufficient vitamin B1 from a varied diet, although it is often added to feed as a supplement to be certain.

Vitamin B2 (riboflavin) is found in milk, green vegetables, and wheat grain. This vitamin acts as a coenzyme in the metabolism of carbohydrates and fats. It, too, is important during pregnancy, and a deficiency can lead to disorders of the nervous system and paralysis.

Vitamin B6 (pyridoxine) is necessary for the absorption and metabolism of amino acids. It is also important in the metabolism of carbohydrates. This vitamin can also be created in the gut.

Vitamin B12 (cobalamin) is important to work in conjunction with other vitamins and amino acids. It is found in food derived from animals and is important for growth. It helps to prevent embryonic disorders and pernicious anemia.

A deficiency can lead to a reduced appetite and growth, make an animal restless and irritable, cause disorders of the nervous system and intestines, loss of condition in the coat, infertility, and sometimes even paralysis.

Vitamin C

Vitamin C (ascorbic acid) is so important for guinea pigs that an entire chapter (Chapter 6) has been devoted to the subject. Guinea pig food should contain 20.5 grains per pound (3,000 mg per kilogram) of vitamin C.

Vitamin D

Vitamin D3 (cholecalciferol) is found in animal fat, fish, meat, cod-liver oil, milk, egg yolks, and vegetables. Through the ultra-violet light in sunshine, the guinea pig can produce this vitamin itself in its skin. Vitamin D is important for the metabolism of calcium and phosphorus and the development of the bone structure. It also plays a role during pregnancy. A deficiency of vitamin D can cause rickets, leading to insufficient calcium, crooked bones, and jawbone deformities. Guinea pig food contains about 900 IU per pound (2,000 IU per kilogram) of vitamin D3.

Vitamin E

Vitamin E (tocopherol) is found in green vegetables, and vegetable oils such as corn (maize), and wheat germ. It is important to the functioning of the immune system and for brain function. The vitamin also helps to prevent food from decaying. A deficiency of vitamin E can lead to paralysis and cause problems in the development of embryos. It can manifest itself with brain and nervous system disorders but muscle and tendon deformities can result, causing paralysis. The vitamin is important in the rearing of rapidly-growing young guinea pigs. In these circumstances supplementary vitamin E can be necessary. Guinea pig food normally contains 0.8 grains per pound (120 mg per kilogram) of vitamin E.

Vitamin K

Vitamin K (phyllochinon) is a complex of vitamins, like vitamin B. Vitamin K3 ensures the coagulation of the blood. It is

A smooth-haired, red and white guinea pig surrounded by vitamin-rich food

found in green plants, soya, meat- and fish-mealfishmeal, milk powder, and alfalfa. Treatment with sulphonamides can have a harmful effect on vitamin K3. A deficiency of this vitamin can lead to internal and sub-cutaneous hemorrhages. Although guinea pigs can produce this vitamin themselves in the large intestine, it is desirable to have 0.08 grains per pound (12 mg per kilogram) of this vitamin in guinea pig food.

Remember that vitamins A, D, E, and K are soluble in fat, while B and C are water soluble. This is important in connection with the manner in which these vitamins are provided.

Minerals

Small amounts of minerals are necessary for the healthy development of the body and the body's chemistry. Guinea pigs mainly derive minerals from vegetable matter. Plants absorb minerals from the ground in which they grow.

Guinea pig food contains about nine percent minerals, of which the important ones are iron, calcium, manganese, and zinc. Calcium, phosphorus, magnesium, chlorine, and copper

Mixed guinea pig food must always be supplemented with a rich source of vitamin C

are also important, and traces of iodine, selenium, and cobalt are required. Calcium and phosphorus are important for their role in laying down calcium in the bone structure. The requirements for these minerals are closely related to the animal's circumstances. Young, pregnant, or suckling animals need greater amounts than others. The greater the demand on the body, the higher the need for these minerals. The ratio between calcium and phosphorus should be about one to a half (1:0.5).

Sodium is needed for the bodily fluids and is to be found in the blood system and lymph glands. Iodine is needed for a good metabolism and the regulation by the hormones of the thyroid. It is also important for growth and its role during reproduction and pregnancy.

Manganese promotes general good health, fertility, and functioning of the nervous system.

Iron and copper are essential trace elements that are especially important for the formation of the hemoglobin, the red oxygen-carrying protein in the blood.

Generally speaking, a lack of certain minerals can create health problems. Proper guinea pig food is the best choice for your animals. Only feed rodent or rabbit food with a rich source of vitamin C. The table below compares the nutritional value of guinea pig, rabbit, and rodent foods.

Key to abbreviations:

min.   = minimum
max.   = maximum

Type of feed	min P	min F	max C	max A
Guinea pigs	20%	4,3%	13,3%	5,8%
Rabbit (mixed)	12,5%	4%	14%	7%
Rodent	12,2%	4,2%	12,8%	6,3%

Vitamin units (approx.)	Vit. A IU/lg	Vit. D IU/lb	E grains/lb	Vit. C grains/lb
Guinea pigs	9.000	900	0.8	20.5
Rabbit (mixed)	2.700	158	0.05	0
Rodent	272	0.07	0	0

P   = raw protein
F   = fat
C   = cellulose (fiber)
A   = ash
IU/lb   = International Units per pound
grain/lb   = grains per pound

The constituency of feeds varies from maker to maker. The optimum proportions have been given for this table. There was a considerable variation in the various types of feed analyzed.

5 DIGESTION

Guinea pigs have relatively long intestines because they are herbivores, with wild guinea pigs having slightly longer intestines than pet guinea pigs. During the digestive process, food is constantly being broken down and nutrients absorbed. The digestive and respiratory processes are essential to the absorption of carbohydrates, fats, proteins, and water that are essential for survival. It is important that there is a good balance between the feed provided and the metabolism. Vitamins and minerals play an important part in this respect. The metabolic rate is determined by the thyroid, together with the temperature, accommodation, and food available. The digestive process becomes more rapid then normal during pregnancy.

The digestive process begins in the mouth. The teeth break the food down into smaller pieces and it is mixed with saliva. The food then passes via the gullet to the stomach, where the acidic gastric juices modify it further. After a time, the acidic and partly digested food or chyme, passes to the duodenum and then into the small intestine, where nutrients are absorbed into the bloodstream. Part of the chyme passes into the blind gut, where it remains for between six and twelve hours. Fiber is converted here, so far as is possible, into digestible nutrients. Finally, the excreta pass through the large intestine and rectum to be ejected from the body as elongated droppings. Before this occurs, waste liquid passes through the kidneys to the bladder. This is a quick overview of the digestive system. It is not possible to deal here with the process in greater detail.

Internal organs
of a sow
(right-hand side)
1. Cervix
2. Large intestine
3. Ovary
4. Kidney
5. Liver
6. Lung
7. Heart
8. Stomach
9. Duodenum
10. Large intestine
11. Small intestine
12. Blind gut

Right:
Red and white
Crested

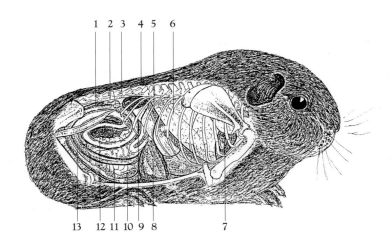

6 THE IMPORTANCE OF VITAMIN C

The most important vitamin for guinea pigs is ascorbic acid, better known as vitamin C. An adequate supply of this vitamin is essential to keep a guinea pig healthy. A deficiency will always cause problems. Humans, apes, and guinea pigs are unable to create vitamin C in the body and are dependent on a minimum quantity being contained in the diet. The scourge of "scurvy" that was suffered by seamen as a result of a deficiency in vitamin C is well-documented. The cause was lack of fresh food containing this essential vitamin.

Cauliflower, cicory, kale and peppers: great sources of vitamin C

Novice keepers or breeders of guinea pigs often find their animals suffer from this problem, which is caused by an incorrect or insufficiently varied diet. If your guinea pig is solely fed mixed rabbit food, it will not have adequate nutrients. A non-branded "guinea pig food" can also lead to similar problems, especially if the guinea pig does not eat all the food it is given because it does not find it appetizing. A guinea pig's diet must be varied. Make sure the guinea pig empties its feeding bowl before you give it fresh feed. There is more information in Chapter 4 about a correct diet.

What are vitamins?

Vitamins are organic compounds that are essential in small quantities to the health and nutrition of most animals. A variety of disorders can manifest themselves by a deficiency or lack of vitamins, generically known as vitamin deficiency. The opposite of this is hypo-vitaminose, which occurs when an excess of certain vitamins is given. This, too, can be harmful, especially if the vitamins are A, D, E, or K. An excess of these vitamins is absorbed into the body's fat. If this food reserve is drawn upon in an emergency, overly high levels of the vitamins can enter the bloodstream and be processed by the kidneys, upsetting the body's nutritional balance. Vitamin C and vitamin B complex are soluble in water and directly absorbed into the bloodstream, with any excess being processed by the kidneys. These vitamins cannot build up in the body over a period of time like the others. Consequently, a deficiency can occur very quickly if there is insufficient vitamin C and B in the diet.

Symptoms of vitamin deficiency

When vitamin C has been missing from the diet for two to four weeks, the first symptoms of vitamin deficiency can be seen. Where the problem is too little vitamin C in the diet, the effects will take longer to manifest themselves. It is known that stress, or a sudden change in circumstances can materially affect the absorption of vitamin C. When there is a deficiency, the animal will become thinner, quickly lose condition, and walk with difficulty. It will lie on its side more frequently to take the pressure off the rear of the body and hind legs. The hair stands up more and the glint goes from the eyes. The swelling of the joints can result in the hindquarters being so badly affected that the animal walks with a limp. Reproduction is not normal with vitamin C deficiency, and pregnancy is unlikely. Young animals do not grow properly and exhibit both skin and coat problems. Spontaneous hemorrhaging occurs, especially in the mucous membranes, and this can cause anemia. Other symptoms include infected gums, discoloration, and loss of teeth. Sudden death of pregnant sows or birth of stillborn offspring also occurs. Inflammation of the intestines, diarrhea, and respiratory problems can be caused by a deficiency in vitamin C, but can occur from other causes. If vitamin deficiency lasts for any time, the guinea pig will die.

Deficiency and causes

Research has shown that guinea pigs that receive some vitamins every day are healthier than those that get them once per week. There are various causes of vitamin deficiency. Insufficient vitamins can only result from poor feeding, such as mixed rabbit and rodent feeds that are not varied enough, too little or the wrong sorts of green fodder, or fodder that is

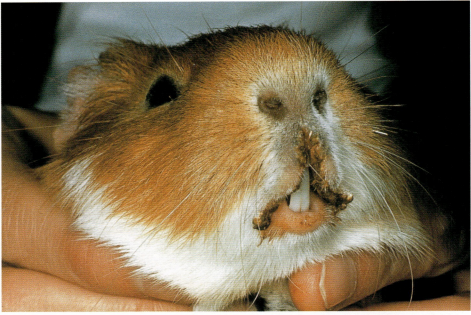

Gum disorder can result from a deficiency of either vitamin A and/or C.

too old and has become too warm so that it contains little by way of vitamins.

Other causes can be a reduced appetite due to illness, or dental problems as a result of insufficient variety in the diet. Problems with the teeth can be congenital abnormalities. These animals should not be bred from because of the suffering that abnormalities of the teeth can cause.

There are circumstances in which a guinea pig will require extra vitamin C. Guinea pigs can suffer vitamin deficiency when in season, because of their age, during pregnancy, or due to stress. Stress can be caused by:
• Too high a density of guinea pigs in a communal cage

- Disturbance due to frequent changes in their regime
- Moving them to new homes or changing temperatures
- Extensive exhibition at shows
- Weaning of young guinea pigs

The consequence of stress and pregnancy is that higher doses of vitamin C are required. The amount available in these circumstances should therefore be larger than normal. The extent of the normal demand for vitamin C of a guinea pig is illustrated by the following example. A human weighing 154lb (70 kg) has a daily requirement of 1.125 grains (75mg) vitamin C, while a guinea pig weighing 2lb 3 oz (1kg) needs at least 0.3 grains (20mg) per day. If the guinea pig gets less than this, problems are almost certain to occur. The demand for vitamin C can be greater under different circumstances. In laboratories where guinea pigs are used as research animals, they work on the following basis:

A pregnant sow needs more vitamin C than normal.

Growing stage or age	Number x the basic requirement (0.3 grains/)
Fully grown adult (maintenance dose)	1 x
Final weeks of pregnancy	2^1/$_2$x
After giving birth, while suckling, and shortly afterward	4^1/$_2$x
Newly-born to mature young	3 x
Breeding specimens	2^1/$_2$x

By knowing the demand for vitamin C, it is possible to establish a responsible level in the diet. This can be done with the help of the nutritional information on the label of the foodstuff. In addition to the dry matter, fat, protein, fiber, and ash, vitamin content is also provided. Ordinary rodent feeds generally contain too little vitamin C for guinea pigs. Special feeds for guinea pigs are fortified with supplementary vitamin C.

Vitamin supplements are also to be found in chinchilla food and feeds intended for young rabbits. It is better to buy regular supplies of feed than to keep a large quantity for a long time, because the vitamin content reduces significantly when the feed is more than three months old. It should be stored in dry and cool conditions for the same reason.

In addition to dry food, green foodstuffs can be good sources of vitamin C. Members of the brassica family, such as kale and cabbage, are first-class sources of vitamin C.

On page 41, a table compares the amount of vitamin C per 3.5 oz (100 g) of various types of fruit and vegetables.

Vegetable/fruit	Grains (mg) of vitamin C per 3.5 oz (100 g) portion
Apple	0.15–0.18 (10–12)
Broccoli	1.7 (113)
Brussels sprouts	2.25 (150)
Carrot	0.08 (5)
Cauliflower	1.05–1.2 (70–80)
Chicory	1.71 (114)
Dandelion leaves	0.52 (35)
Endive	0.15 (10)
Green cabbage	1.2 (80)
Green cucumber	0.15 (10)
Kale	1.5–1.88 (100–125)
Orange	0.75 (50)
Parsley	2.58 (172)
Pear	0.06 (4)
Peppers	1.5–2.25 (100–150)
Rose hips	7.5 (500)
Spinach	0.38–0.75 (25–50)
Strawberry	0.9 (60)
Tomatoes	0.38 (25)

A varied diet is also essential for keeping young guinea pigs healthy.

Note that, although the vitamin C content of endives, cucumbers, apples, pears, and carrots is low, these are still excellent foods for guinea pigs. The table on page 41 shows that a guinea pig would need to eat excessive amounts of certain foods to derive its vitamin requirement. Grass is another first-class source of vitamin C, but the amount of vitamin C can vary greatly from day to day.

Alternative sources of vitamin C

There are other ways in which vitamin C can be provided:

- Effervescent vitamin C tablets as required
- Vitamin drops containing various vitamins and trace elements. Use these drops as a dietary supplement
- Vitamin tablets that have to be dissolved in water
- Rose-hip syrup

The offspring of Peruvian guinea pigs are born with long hairs that grow longer with time.

The provision of vitamin C via the drinking water requires some experience, because it is not very easy to assess how much each guinea pig drinks. The effectiveness of vitamin C is also short-lived when dissolved in water.

The main points from this chapter are:
- Guinea pigs cannot produce vitamin C in their bodies.
- The demand for vitamin C is great but varies according to circumstances.
- The vitamin C requirement should be provided by a varied and balanced diet.
- A varied diet is of great importance.

Green fodder is a good source of vitamin C.

7 CARING FOR A GUINEA PIG

Proper care for a guinea pig requires daily attention and thought for the behavior and welfare of the animal. It is important that the guinea pig is held firmly but correctly. To pick a guinea pig up, first place a hand under the front legs and support the hindquarters with the other hand (see illustration). By this means, the entire body is supported, which prevents the guinea pig from wriggling free and falling. Never pick a guinea pig up with one hand around the back of the neck and rib cage—it will find this very threatening, as though it has been captured by a predator.

Because guinea pigs are rodents, their teeth need to be routinely checked; their claws require regular clipping, too. It goes without saying that the cage or hutch must be kept clean. A thin layer of sawdust covered by sweet-smelling fresh hay makes an ideal litter for the guinea pig's home. Make sure there is sufficient hay so that the guinea pig can hide in it. Straw is not suitable because it is too hard and coarse.

An earthenware bowl will suffice as a feeding dish. Provided guinea pigs are introduced to it when young, a water bottle is more suitable than a drinking bowl because water in a bottle will not become soiled so quickly. Make sure that the water is not exposed all day to the sun, and provide a fresh supply every day. Some people insist that guinea pigs do not drink. This is not true! Their thirst can be particularly great if they are only fed with dry fodder such as guinea pig food or pellets, and also when they are suckling young. Provided they have access to ample grass or green fodder, the demand for water diminishes. The final part of the daily care is to provide a rack of fresh hay and/or green fodder.

Grooming of guinea pigs requires a great deal of attention, and incorporates checking for unwanted intruders in the coat. Grooming is even more important in the cases of Abyssinian, Silkie, Peruvian, and Texel guinea pigs.

Some guinea pigs lose hair all the time because of the temperature at which they are kept. This can also be caused by incorrect diet. Guinea pigs should not be housed in conditions that are too warm and, if they are kept indoors, they must certainly not be close to central heating radiators or other sources of heat, or placed in the full sun. A well-balanced diet prevents hair loss. Quite a lot of guinea pigs are given overfilled bowls of mixed rabbit or rodent food and eat just those bits they find tasty, leaving

Right: This is the best way to pick up a guinea pig.

their owners to throw away the rest. This results in an insufficiently varied diet. If you do give a guinea pig rabbit or rodent food (about 1¹/₃–1¹/₂ oz /40–50 g per day), you must first ensure that it has all been eaten before you give the guinea pig any more. If this is not done, hair loss is likely to occur through malnutrition. Such rabbit and rodent feeds must always be supplemented with additional vitamin C. Some guinea pigs are fussy about what they eat and refuse certain foods. This problem is almost unheard of if special guinea pig food is provided.

The hair needs to be well but carefully brushed before wrapping it in "curlers."

Returning to the matter of hair loss, this is not normally a problem with smooth-haired guinea pigs. Brushing their coats from time to time is sufficient. Those with an unusual coat,

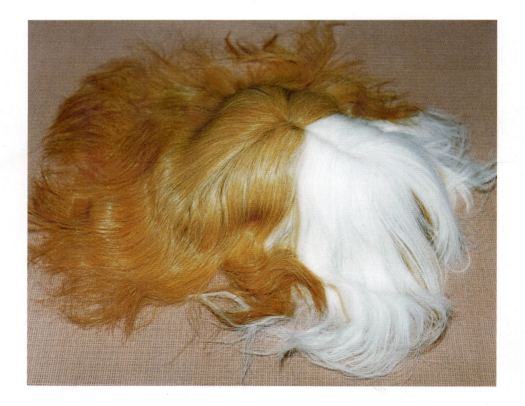

however, require more care. Texel, Abyssinian, and Rex guinea pigs will require more frequent grooming. Peruvian and Silkies need special grooming. These varieties are really only suitable for keeping by real enthusiasts or breeders who can devote a great deal of time to their animals. Tangles can occur in the coat because of its length. Do not torture the animal by trying to comb these out; clipping is the only solution.

Breeders often wrap the hair in paper to keep it from tangling. These wrappers are removed for showing the animals in their full glory. Rolling the hair up in these wrappers prevents it from becoming dirty and entangled with pieces of hay. The special wrappers are available in a range of sizes for different lengths of hair. To wrap the hair in this way, the following items are needed.

- A strong piece of rectangular paper, twice as long as the "curler."
- A piece of lightweight wood about 1/12–1/6 in. (2–4mm) thick and 5/8–2 in. (1.5–5cm) long to use as the "curler."
- A roll of adhesive tape.
- An elastic band.

The step-by-step process of wrapping the hair is then done as follows:

- Cut a piece of paper so that it is twice the width of the piece of wood.
- Fold about 5/8 in. (1.5 cm) of the top of the paper over.
- Place the piece of wood in the middle of the paper, beneath the fold.
- Tape this down with the adhesive tape.
- Fold the outside edges of the paper vertically over to close it so that the folds line up with the ends of the stick.
- Fasten this with an elastic band
- Leave for several hours.
- Once the creases are firmly marked, you can unfold the paper.

The wrappers are fastened to Peruvian guinea pigs as described next.

- Brush the guinea pig and part the hair cleanly along the center of the back.
- At the hindquarters, there will be two rosettes of hair. Brush the hair from these toward the rear of the animal.
- Place a wooden "curler" along each side of the guinea pig and one behind the hindquarters.
- Lay the hair on the paper and place the piece of wood against the roots of the hairs.
- Now roll each paper wrap up and fasten with the elastic band to keep it in position.

With Silkies, two separate wrappers are used on each side, and one for the hair over the hindquarters (in front of the train). Once the hair has been wrapped, make sure that the animal is not uncomfortable before placing it back in its hutch.

*First roll up the
hair on each of
the sides.*

*Lay a strand of
hair on the paper.*

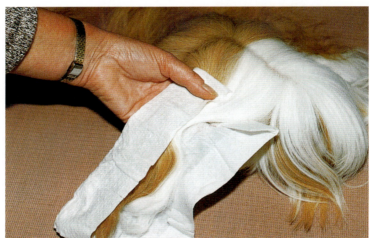

*Fold the paper
closed.*

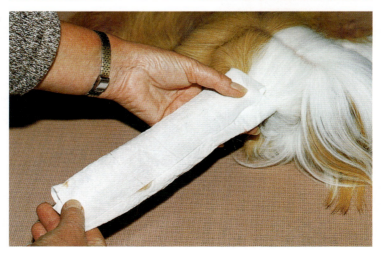

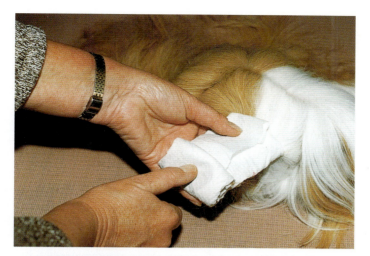

Loosely roll up the paper.

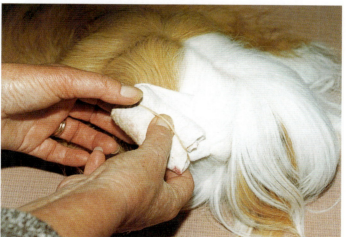

Fasten the wrapper with an elastic band.

Repeat the process with the hindquarters.

8 BREEDING GUINEA PIGS

Right: Young Texel guinea pigs have their attractive curly hair soon after birth.

It is not essential to breed guinea pigs in order to enjoy keeping them, but breeding does heighten the enjoyment. Some enthusiasts breed in order to show their offspring and have them judged against the breed standards. Chapter 13 has more about the rewards of competitive showing of guinea pigs.

Before breeding a litter of guinea pigs, it is best to make sure that you can find homes for them. If this is not the case, then do not breed your animals. Guinea pigs are sexually mature at an early age, so, if you wish to avoid offspring, you must keep the boars separated from the sows. If not, the females will be pregnant almost permanently.

The differences between the sexes can be seen at a young age: left, a sow; right, a boar.

Male guinea pigs are known as boars and the females as sows. It is more difficult to differentiate the sexes in young animals and this requires some experience. Some of the differences between the two sexes are:
- The space between the anus and sexual organ is smaller with sows than with boars (see illustration);
- Young boars grow more rapidly than sows;

- Adult boars are always larger and more robustly built than sows;
- The testicles can be felt at an age of a few weeks old with boars and, by pressing the sexual orifice, the penis can be made to appear;
- The behavior of sows changes when they are in season; they become more affectionate and boisterous.

Mating guinea pigs are rarely seen because they are somewhat "prudish"

Differentiating between small males and females does need some experience. It might be possible to get help from an experienced breeder. Some boars become sexually mature at a very young age, much earlier than the sows. It is therefore best to separate the sexes not later than four weeks old. Young males can be bred from at three months old. Females become sexually mature at about eight to ten weeks, but this does not mean that a young sow is ready to be covered. Such a young sow is still too young and immature for breeding. Experience has shown that the best age for covering a sow is around five

months old. If the first mating occurs later than this, the sow is less likely to become pregnant and problems can occur, both in giving birth and rearing the young. The litter is often bigger, but there may be less milk. A guinea pig remains in season for 17–18 days. Her behavior toward males is then distinctive. The best moment may only last a few hours and this is not so easy to determine. During the season, the membrane in the vagina breaks, making mating possible. Once the moment has passed, the membrane reforms until the next occasion the female is in season. Mating is rarely seen because it is preceded by an extended period of courtship and because guinea pigs are somewhat "prudish." During the pregnancy, especially during the second half of gestation, the sow's nutritional needs increase. During this time, she has an increased demand for vitamin C, and it is important that the basis of her diet is a complete guinea pig food.

A certain amount of influence can be had on the size of the litter. It was discovered by coincidence that slim guinea pigs that are given plenty of food for two weeks before mating, thus making them grow, produce more offspring than if in their normal condition. Fat, overfed guinea pigs are difficult to

A red marked Dutch guinea pig with young

breed successfully, less likely to become pregnant, and often experience difficult births. Newly-born guinea pigs are delivered with hair and open eyes, so that they can flee the nest if necessary. They also have teeth.

The gestation period is fairly lengthy: on average between 66 and 72 days, mainly influenced by age, condition, and diet. In the wild, guinea pigs give birth to their young in a grassy lair, rather like hares. In captivity, they will often happily give birth within the group. It is better, however, at the end of the pregnancy, to segregate the sow in a hutch that is supplied with plenty of good hay. Birth normally takes no longer than twenty to thirty minutes, with on average two to three guinea pigs being born shortly after each other. Larger litters are possible and do not necessarily pose problems. The young guinea pigs weigh $2^{4}/_{5}$–$4^{1}/_{4}$ oz (80–120 g) at birth. Although the sow only has two nipples, her milk supply is adequate for even four or five youngsters. It is best not to leave the male with the female because she quickly comes into season, sometimes even within hours of giving birth.

It is always surprising to see newly-born guinea pigs wandering around full of curiosity with their eyes open. Although the young suckle their mother until they are about four weeks old, they start to search for solid food within days of their birth. Once the peak milk production has passed with the mother, this will happen even more. The animals are able to feed themselves totally about 25 days after the birth. Young sows can be removed from their mother when they are five or six weeks old. If this is done earlier, the guinea pigs are likely to find the break too abrupt. Some breeders suggest that the young can be removed at three weeks, but this really is not advisable; it is, however, recommended that the boars be taken away at four weeks, because some of them may be capable of mating and causing unwanted pregnancies. There are also some strange ideas about the number of litters a guinea pig can cope with in a year. Two litters each year are more than enough. It is physically possible for a sow to have more litters but this would be at the expense of her welfare.

*Multi-colored
Peruvian*

*[p55 bottom]
The young should
not be removed
from their mother
too soon*

Right: red-marked
Dutch guinea pigs

[p56 bottom]
From left to right:
Himalayan, Lilac,
Abyssinian
Harlequin,
American Crested,
Dalmatian, Golden
Satin, Beige, and
Abyssinian Brindle.
Photograph from
Avicultura,
December 1994,
courtesy of the
publishers Delta
Press BV

9 BREEDS, VARIETIES, AND CHOICE OF BREED

The number of possible guinea pig breeds and varieties has grown so much in the past 15 years or so that it might perhaps be difficult for a newcomer to decide which breed to choose. Not all of the breeds are suitable for keeping by the inexperienced enthusiast and it is better to gain some practice with normal guinea pigs before considering a Silkie or Texel. A local local guinea pig club can give pointers and advise about breeders in your area. The great diversity of varieties and colorings that now exist are described in brief in this chapter. In general terms, guinea pigs can be divided into two groups:

A. Guinea pigs with normal hair, also known as smooth-haired.

B. Guinea pigs with unusual types of hair, such as:
   • Crested guinea pigs
   • Abyssinian (wire-haired)
   • Peruvian (long-haired)
   • Silkies
   • Satin Coated
   • Rex Coated
   • Texel Coated

Colors and markings

Guinea pigs in all the varieties listed above come in a wide range of colorings. These are sub-divided as follows:
• Agouti or wild coloring;
• Single-colored, known as Self-colored;
• Marked guinea pigs with up to three colors.

In the breed descriptions, you will often come across the term "ticking." Guinea pigs with ticking in their coats are agouti-colored, with outer hairs that are not single colored but consist of various colors. These colors are dispersed in bands on each hair of light and dark colors next to each other. The term "undercolor" refers to the hair next to the body. "Top color" refers to the color of the outer part of the hairs that is most visible. There is no uniformity of breed standards internationally, and not every breed or variety is recognized in every country.

Agouti

Agouti guinea pigs have markings that are typical of wild guinea pigs. This is seen at its clearest with Golden Agouti specimens. With the Gray, Silver, and Golden Agouti breeds, the undercolor is blue-black with an overlay of the main color in bands on parts of the hair. The agouti marking results from the fact that some of the undercolor appears on the outer part of the hairs, making them partially black. The ticking should be uniformly spread across the entire body, except on the belly where the hairs have less of the undercolor ticking, with pure, unmodified top color. The following agouti colors are recognized:

Golden Agouti: The original guinea pig coloring, which is a warm chestnut/reddish brown with regular black ticking. This is found on the legs, chest, head, and around the eyes. The undercolor of the top coat and sides of the belly is blue-black. There is no ticking on the belly. The claws, soles of the feet, and ears are black, while the eyes should be as dark brown as possible.

Gray Agouti: A buff-colored coat with regular black ticking over the entire body except the belly. The undercolor of the top coat and belly is a blue-black. The claws, pads, and ears are black, while the eyes are dark brown. This color is difficult to

Golden Agouti

breed true, due to the influence of Silver Agouti and Buff and Cream guinea pigs.

Gray Agouti

Silver Agouti: Characterized by the silver-gray top color with black ticking, which is missing from the belly. The undercolor of the top coat and belly is blue-black. The claws, pads, and ears are black. Dark brown eyes are preferable.

Cinnamon Agouti: A silver-white top color with even, cinnamon-colored ticking and a silver-white belly. The undercolor of the belly and top coat is cinnamon. The ears and pads are light brown, with brown claws. The dark brown eyes reflect sparkling red when viewed from certain angles.

Silver Agouti

Cinnamon Agouti

Argente: A pinkish salmon color. The ticking is formed by lilac-colored tips to the hairs. The belly is salmon pink, and the undercolor of the top coat and belly is lilac. The ears and pads are flesh-colored, without any pigmentation, with natural horn-colored claws. The bright pink eye color is striking.

Self-colors

The single-color of Self breeds forms an important group. Breeding fine specimens of single-color guinea pigs that meet the breed standard is a great challenge for many breeders.

Argente

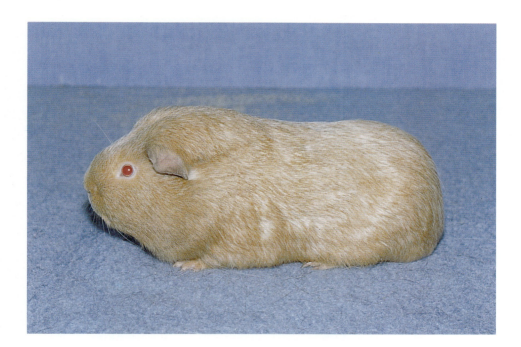

The Self Black guinea pig has hairs that are shiny black from tip to skin, although the hairs on the belly are somewhat less lustrous. Other colors such as red and white hairs sometimes occur, but these are regarded as a fault. The ears, feet, pads, and claws are black, with dark brown eyes.

Self Chocolate guinea pigs have a shiny coat that is an even, dark brown (the color of plain chocolate) over the entire body. The outer hair should be as dark as possible. The ears, pads, and feet are dark brown, the claws are brown, and the eyes, which are

Self Black

dark brown, sparkle warm red when viewed from a particular angle. The challenge with this breed is to produce animals that have an even color over their entire coat, without changes in tint.

Self Chocolate

Self Lilac guinea pigs are very attractive, with an even coat that is light blue with a rosy tinge. This rosy tinge should not be too dark. The hairs are the same color from tip to skin, but the

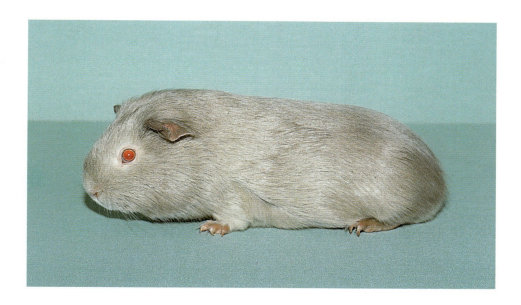

color is somewhat duller on the belly. The ears and pads are flesh colored, with natural horn-colored claws and red eyes. Breeding the correct color is quite difficult, but this is why this breed appeals to some enthusiasts. There is a relationship between Self Lilac and Self Beige guinea pigs.

Self Lilac

Self Beige guinea pigs are a dark cream with a hint of gray, but this must not verge on brown. The color should be even across the entire body, but with a matte appearance on the belly. The

Self Beige

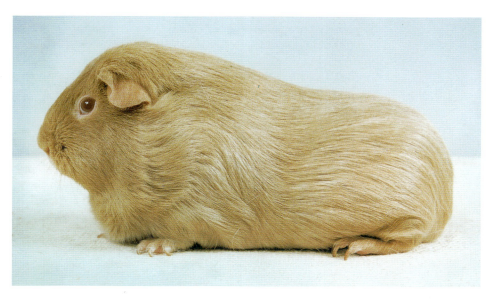

ears and pads are flesh-colored, with natural horn-colored nails and red eyes. There is a relationship between Self Beige and Self Lilac guinea pigs.

Self Red guinea pigs are a warm chestnut/reddish-brown, without any lighter or darker hairs or ticking. Lighter hair on the flanks is fairly common, but this is a fault. The belly is

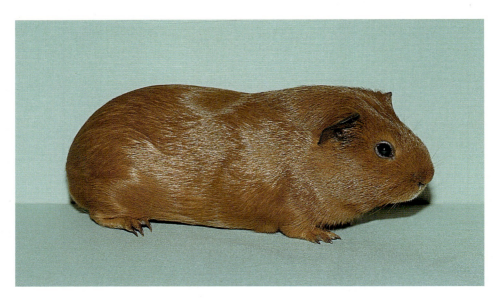

Self Red   duller in coloring. The ears are without pigment but the pads are black, while the claws are dark horn-colored and the eyes brown. A pure Self Red guinea pig is a feast for the eyes. Newly-born guinea pigs often fail to display the correct color; this can only be assessed when they are older.

Self Golden is really a warmish orange that is the same color over the entire body, but slightly duller on the belly. There are Dark-Eyed Goldens and Pink-Eyed Goldens.

Buff has a dark yellow ocher coloring (rather like that of a chamois leather), which should not err on the red side. The ears and pads are flesh-colored and preferably without pigmentation, but this is not always the case. The claws are horn-colored and the eyes are brown-black. This breed is classified as a rare variety, but is included with the Self-colored breeds because it is a single, uniform color.

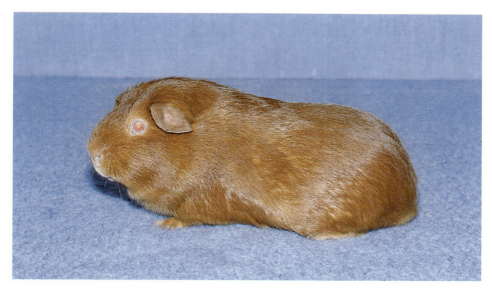

Self Golden

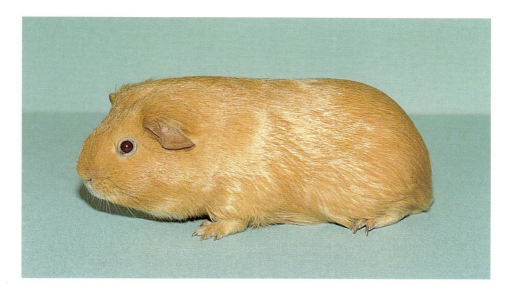

Buff

Self Cream guinea pigs should have an even tone over their entire body, except for the belly, which is slightly duller. The ears and pads are flesh-colored, with horn-colored claws and brown eyes. The breeding of a first-class example of a Self Cream is extremely difficult, with the color often not coming true. Regular inbreeding between Self Cream guinea pigs can result in the offspring becoming more buff-colored, which makes outcrossing with white necessary.

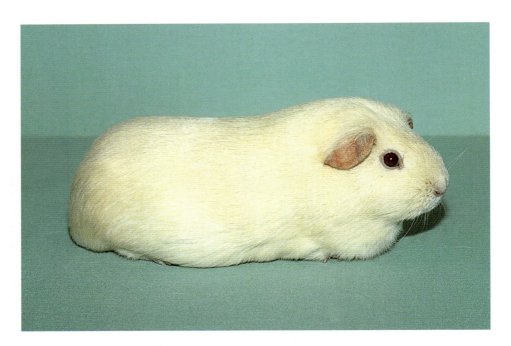

Self Cream

Dark-eyed Self White

Self White guinea pigs are recognized in two varieties: Dark-eyed White and Pink-eyed White. The Dark-eyed Self White has a snow whitesnow-white coat without a hint of any other color. The ears and pads should be flesh-colored and the claws without pigmentation. The eyes are brown or blue. These

guinea pigs are not genetically albino, since they bear the gene for color that is apparent from the eyes. The Pink-eyed Self White is an albino and identical in appearance, except for the color of the eyes. Self White guinea pigs when bred can produce guinea pigs of various colors. Self White guinea pigs are generally sound animals and tend to be larger than average.

Pink-eyed Self White

Marked breeds

Brindle guinea pigs have flecks of red and black regularly distributed across the body. The colors should not form spots or patches, and the inclusion of other colors, which often occurs, is regarded as a fault. The ears and pads are black, with claws preferably dark brown to black, although natural horn color also occurs. The eyes are dark brown. The coloring of Brindles is similar to Tortoiseshell and Harlequin, but the colors of these coats are more sharply defined.

Tortoiseshell guinea pigs have sharply defined red and black markings, with a preference for rectangular shapes. The markings should be formed in such a way that the opposing halves of the body have different colors, with a clear division along the center of the back. The ears and pads are black, with claws that are as dark as possible. The eyes are very dark brown. It goes without saying that breeding this type true requires significant experience and dedication.

Tortoiseshell and white guinea pigs have evenly distributed, same-sized spots of these colors, all three of which should appear on each side of the body. The eyes should be dark and the ears and pads should be a similar color to that of the surrounding hair.

Bicolor and Tricolor guinea pigs are two or three colors, other than those of a Tortoiseshell. The markings must be clearly defined, with the right balance between the colors and white.

Harlequin guinea pigs are even more complicated than Tortoiseshells. The colors are as Tortoiseshell but instead are arranged in bands around the head. Where the right-hand side is red, the left is then black. There must be a dark ear on the red half of the head and a red ear on the black half. The colors are delineated down the middle of the back and belly. The Harlequin is so difficult to breed that only a limited number of breeders are attracted to it.

Dutch guinea pigs have similar markings to Dutch rabbits, with the same color on both sides of the head and a white blaze in between, which are characteristic of the breed. The rear third of the body shares the same color as the head. The front

legs are white but the hind legs have white socks. The dark eye color is related to the color other than white of the coat, and the pads have no pigmentation. The recognized colors are black, chocolate, red, or agouti. These markings are difficult to breed true and present a major challenge to enthusiasts.

Smooth-haired Tricolor

Black Dutch

Group of Himalayans

Himalayan guinea pigs are pure white with an attractively rounded dark mask (nose), and the same color ears, feet, and pads. The claws are black, but the eyes are pink. There are two varieties of Himalayan: with either black or chocolate markings.

Bicolor and Tricolor guinea pigs are two or three colors other than the red and black, or red, black, and white of Tortoiseshell and Tortoiseshell and white. The markings must be clearly defined, with the right balance between the colors and white.

Unusual types of coat

Crested guinea pigs

Crested guinea pigs originated in the United States and are sometimes classified into two types: the American Crested and English Crested.

Peruvian guinea pig with superb color markings

English Crested have a rosette of hair in the center of the forehead, slightly forward of the ears and between the eyes. The rosette is the same color as the rest of the body, which is of one color. The rosette is rounded and should be as large as possible, radiating out from a small center. Crests are appearing on all manner and variety of guinea pig, but only certain types are officially recognized at the present time.

American Crested have a white rosette that contrasts with the color of the rest of the body, which is generally black, red, golden, or buff. At present, Crested guinea pigs are all

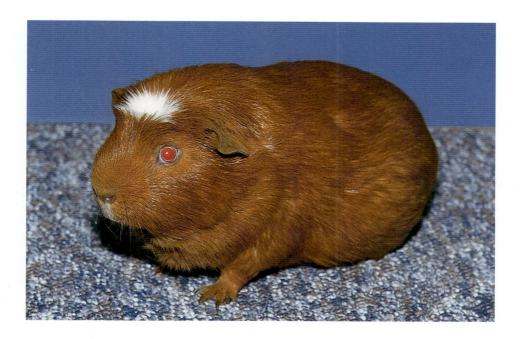

smooth-haired, but enthusiasts are developing Crested with all manner of types. It is important when buying a Crested to ensure that the rosette has only one center; a double centered or divided rosette is a hereditary fault.

Abyssinian or Wire-haired
Abyssinian guinea pigs have hair that is about 1⅓ in. (3.5 cm) long with their bodies being covered in rosettes, which should each be as large as possible, but not touching each other. The ideal standard is four large rosettes in a line, with a rosette on each hip and one each on the shoulders and hindquarters. Finally, there should be a rosette on the nose or mask. Between the rosettes, there should be combs of hair standing up where the rosettes come close to each other. The shape and form of the rosettes are more important than the number of them. The hair on the head should look all askew and beards are highly desirable.

Peruvian or Long-haired
Peruvian guinea pigs have very long, dense, lustrous hair that is springy and soft to the touch. When not wrapped to protect it, the hair hangs down over the face and bottom so that it can be difficult to see which is the front and back of a guinea pig. The hair that falls over the eyes is formed in a rosette or whorl, and the hair is parted along the back to fall across the animal's

American Crested guinea pig

Left:
Cream English Crested boar

Satin Coated Abyssinian guinea pig

sides. Whorls on the hips cause the hair to fall in a "train." Daily grooming is essential to keep the coat of this breed in good condition and to prevent it from tangling. It is very demanding in terms of time to brush the guinea pig regularly. Before shows, this breed usually has its coat protected by wrapping the hair in paper, to prevent it from developing tangles. Some national standards have set colors. This breed is sometimes known as a Long-haired, but in some countries Longhair is considered as a breed category incorporating Peruvian, Coronet, Silkie, and Texel.

Peruvian

Silkies or Shelties

Silkies (sometimes known as Shelties) are a pure long-haired guinea pig in which the rosettes or whorls have been bred out. Although Silkies are bred intentionally, they can also occur spontaneously in a litter of Peruvians. Because there are no whorls, the train fans out from the rump. The long, dense, soft, springy hair hangs down the sides like a mane. The hair is normal length on the mask and there are beards on the cheeks. The longer hair begins between the eyes and ears and runs into the beards. Colors can vary from country to country, but red, black, white, tricolor, tortoiseshell, and roan are all fairly common.

Silkie

Golden Satin Coated

Satin Coated

Satin Coated guinea pigs have normal-length hair that has a satin sheen. The marvellous shine of the hair, which reaches right down to the root, results from a thinning of the hair shaft.

Because the hair is very densely packed, this coat has a special texture that is not instantly apparent. Satin Coated guinea pigs were only recently recognized, and the breed has not existed long. Check with your national guinea pig organization as to which colors and varieties are recognized. Satin Coats have also appeared on Peruvians, creating a new variety that is certain to prove popular with enthusiasts.

Rex Coated

Rex Coated guinea pigs have short, curly hair that is springy and does not lie flat. The breed was developed in the United Kingdom, but because the breed is fairly new, the quality of the animals can vary widely.

Texel

Texel guinea pigs resulted from cross-breedingcrossbreeding the Silkie and Rex. Texels have long curly hair that can be more than 4½ in. (12 cm) long, and there is a wide variety of colors. The belly hairs are fine, with tight curls. Texels are a fairly new breed, but the breed's development is well advanced and there is considerable interest in them.

New breeds

Breeders constantly strive to develop new breeds, not all of which are recognized internationally. The Dalmatian is a fairly new breed, with black spots on a white coat rather like

A new variety: Tricolor Rex

Texel

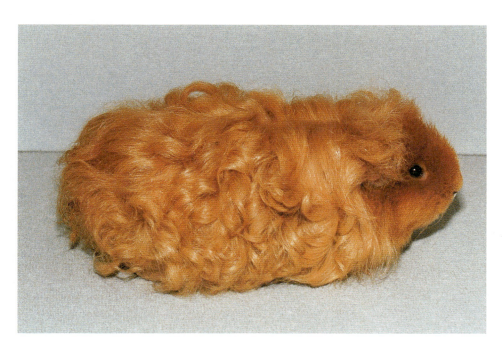

Dalmatian guinea pig

Coronets are really crested Silkies

Dalmatian dogs. The head is often marked with patches. German breeders are particularly active with this breed. The Coronet is a Silkie with a rosette. The breed was developed in Britain. The Merino is a Coronet with a Rex coat, but they are fairly rare. The Alpaca is a Peruvian guinea pig that carries the gene for a Rex coat.

Tricolor Peruvian

10 GENETICS

Right: One of the new varieties: Red Satin-coated Abyssinians

Those who want to breed guinea pigs will need to have an understanding of Mendel's theory of genetics. Much use is made of these "rules" in the breeding of guinea pigs, because different generations can be compared in a short space of time. This chapter only provides an introduction to genetics. For a deeper study of the subject, you will need a specialist book on the subject.

Inherited characteristics are determined by genes and chromosomes. Chromosomes are located in the cells and are surrounded by the cell wall. The protein content of a cell is known as protoplasm. The nucleus of the cell is located within the protoplasm and within this are many colored "grains" or chromatins. These unite in pairs to form chromosomes. Each species of animal and plant has a characteristic number of chromosome pairs. Guinea pigs have 32.

The breeder's skill lies in rearing these Dutch guinea pigs with markings as uniform as possible

In applying genetic theory we are concerned with certain characteristics and to what extent these are genetically inherited,

such as color and type of coat or marking. If you choose to breed guinea pigs, it will be important to find out how these characteristics can be improved within the bounds of genetics. Characteristics are generally genetically dominant, recessive, intermediate, or are linked to gender. It is essential to understand these terms.

Dominant means a characteristic that prevails over other characteristics. Golden Agouti is, for instance, dominant compared with other colors. If this characteristic is in the parents' genes, then the offspring will definitely inherit it. Rosettes, wire-haired coats, and crests are dominant over normal hair, but normal hair is dominant over long hair.

Recessive is the opposite of dominant: Harlequin and Dutch markings are recessive compared with a color, but self colors-self-colors are recessive compared with Golden Agouti.
If the result of cross-breeding falls between the two genetic factors of the parents, it is intermediate. For example, if Buff and Self White guinea pigs are crossed, the result will be cream, a mixture of the two.

Gender dependent means that the inherited characteristic depends on whether the offspring is a sow or boar. In addition to these terms, you may encounter breed true and its opposite, not true breeding. If a characteristic is to be found on the chromosomes of both parents, it will breed true. When this is not the case, the characteristic is not true breeding. Inherited characteristics are passed on genetically, but diet, accommodation, and care can also play a part in the eventual breeding results.

Smooth-haired
Tricolor

11 ANATOMY

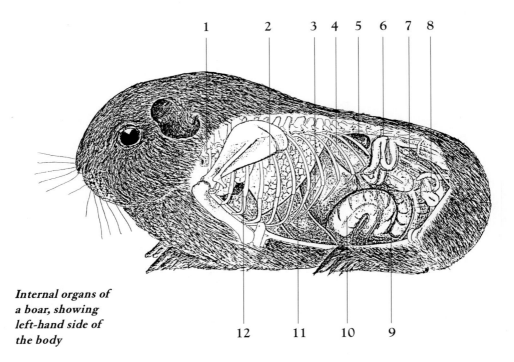

1 2 3 4 5 6 7 8

12 11 10 9

Internal organs of a boar, showing left-hand side of the body

1. Windpipe
2. Lung
3. Stomach
4. Spleen
5. Kidney
6. Large intestine
7. Seminal tube
8. Testis
9. Blind gut
10. Liver
11. Heart

It is best to understand your guinea pig'sguinea pig anatomy. It is not necessary to be able to name every part of the animal, but knowledge of the main anatomical features is always useful. In the healthcare chapter, reference is made to parts of the guinea pig anatomy, and it is helpful to understand what is referred to. The illustrations show the internal organs and external anatomy of smooth-haired guinea pigs, with the different parts named. Some of these terms will be encountered in breed standards, and they are also used for breed descriptions. Because the external appearance of an animal gives important indications to its internal condition, it is sensible to examine the body of a guinea pig thoroughly. Not all guinea pigs are the same, of course—they come in a variety of body types—some colors are more robustly built than others and the lengths also vary. This book is not able to deal with these differences in any detail. If you are interested, it is best to obtain the standard for the breed in question from a recognized guinea pig organization.

The domestication of guinea pigs is of comparatively recent origin, but the consequences can clearly be seen if pet guinea pigs are compared with those born and living wild. Pet guinea pigs are slightly smaller and shorter that wild ones and the digestive system has been modified to cope with a different diet, with the intestines becoming shorter. The coat of pet guinea pigs is softer than that of wild specimens and, with man's involvement, other forms of coat such as Abyssinian, Peruvian, Satin Coated, and Rex have been developed.

A good guinea pig fulfills certain requirements. It feels sturdy to the touch, with a good muscular frame, and has a lively appearance. The build is in proportion, with a fine, fully-developedfully developed, broad and powerful head on a short, strong neck. The space between the eyes and ears should be wide, with a pronounced curve to the mask or nose and well-developed cheeks. The slightly drooping and hairless ears are fleshy, with a slight kink in the middle. The eyes are large, clear, and slightly protruding. The shoulders should be high,

Red and white rossetes

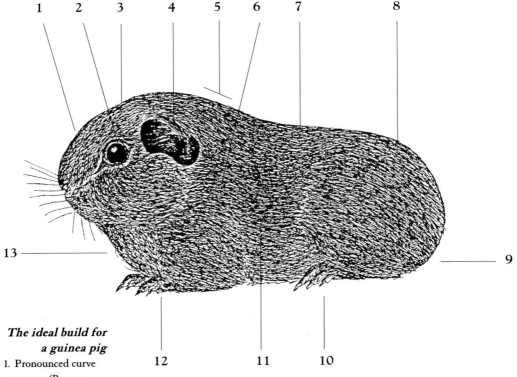

The ideal build for a guinea pig

1. Pronounced curve to nose (Roman nose), well-rounded snout with well-developed cheeks
2. Clear, slightly protruding eyes
3. Face
4. Ears at right-angles to the head, without tears
5. Crest
6. High and wide shoulders
6. Back
7. Well-rounded hindquarters
8. No tail
9. Hind legs
10. Side or flanks
11. Straight and sturdy front or fore legs

broad, and well-muscled, while the chest between the front legs should be broad and firm. The rib cage is well rounded, giving ample room for the various organs. Guinea pigs are short and stockily built, giving an impression of strength. From the shoulder to the hindquarters, the broad, short back falls away slightly and, seen from above, is smaller at the rear than the front. The rear or hindquarters are nicely rounded and well-covered. Guinea pigs do not have tails. The fairly short legs are straight and sturdy; the front feet have four short toes, but the feet on the hind legs have only three. Large, well-proportioned guinea pigs are preferred in the show ring, with the weight dependant on both sex and breed, but in the range 1lb 15 oz–2lb 10 oz (900–1,200 g).

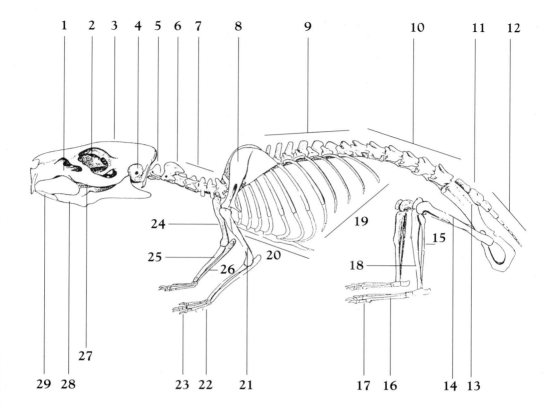

Skeleton

1. Cheekbone
2. Eye socket
3. Skull
4. Ear
5. Atlas (cervical vertebra)
6. Axis
7. Neck vertebrae
8. Collar bone
9. Chest vertebrae
10. Lumber vertebrae
11. Sacrum
12. Tail vertebrae
13. Pelvis (hip bone)
14. Femur (thigh bone)
15. Calf
16. Metatarsus (foot bones)
17. Toes
18. Tibia (shin bone)
19. Floating ribs
20. Ribs
21. Humerus (upper arm bone)
22. Metacarpus (hand bones)
23. Digital phalanx (finger bones)
24. Humerus
25. Radius (spoke bone)
26. Ulna
27. Molars (teeth)
28. Bottom jaw
29. Incisors (teeth)

ANATOMY **89**

12 GUINEA PIG HEALTH CARE

Caring for your guinea pig also includes the prevention, so far as possible, of illness. Guinea pigs appear not to be sick very often, or at least never appear to be ill, but the worrying fact is that, if a guinea pig shows signs of sickness, it is usually too late. In such cases, the little creature will not readily get better and is likely to die quite quickly. Because of this, the owner needs to remain alert to any signs and monitor them constantly. Fortunately, well cared-for guinea pigs do not readily become ill. The greater risks of illness lie with breeders who keep a greater number of guinea pigs than enthusiasts with just the one. Breeders, however, usually have greater experience with animals and can recognize specific diseases more quickly and treat them. Guinea pigs react adversely to modern

Tricolor Peruvian

drugs such as antibiotics, because bacteria in the gut appear to be beneficial to the digestion of food. Treatment with antibiotics can upset the natural balance, so drugs need to be given with great care. Fortunately, there are other drugs that do not cause side effects for guinea pigs. Your veterinarian may need to consult one of the research centers with specialist knowledge of diseases in guinea pigs.

Measures that you can take to prevent illness or detect it quickly include:
- Feed regularly at the same times;
- Start feeding each day with tufts of good quality hay;
- Ensure the diet contains sufficient vitamin C;
- Provide a varied diet without too much reliance on one foodstuff;

- Clean the feeding bowl and drinking bottle daily;
- Clean out the cage or hutch regularly;
- Do not house a guinea pig in the full sun, or exposed to wind and rain;
- Prevent drafts or damp from entering the hutch;
- Carefully note the guinea pig's condition while feeding it. Is it eating properly? Does it look all right? Are the droppings normal? Is the guinea pig active?
- If necessary, check the guinea pig's temperature. The normal temperature should be 99.5–102.2°F (37.5–39°C). Temperatures above this range can be regarded as on the high side or feverish.

If your guinea pig appears to lose condition, it is essential to find out as quickly as possible what the cause is in order to take the necessary action. Do not delay in calling in a vet because, the longer you wait, the more difficult it will be to cure the ani-

Himalayan

Young, marked Peruvian guinea pig

mal. Some illnesses are difficult or even impossible to cure, so try to prevent them. To help you recognize the symptoms of various disorders that can affect guinea pigs, some of the known illnesses are described below.

Abscesses

Although abscesses are not common, they are included to aid their differentiation from tumors, with which they can be confused. There are two types of abscesses: those which result from an external infection via, for example, a wound, and others resulting from an infection in the lymph nodes of the head and/or stomach. The first type is limited to one at the seat of the infection. The second type will usually affect more than one guinea pig if there is a group. The illness comes and goes but symptoms appear rapidly. It is essential to isolate the infected animals, and the vet should be called to ascertain if the abscesses are of the infectious kind. Sometimes it is necessary to lance and disinfect an abscess if it does not burst of its own accord, together with a course of drugs. Abscesses can also occur under the pads of older guinea pigs, which can recur after treatment or even become chronic.

Coccidiosis

Coccidiosis is a disorder in which parasitic protozoa damage the lining of the intestines. They can survive outside the body as oocytes (immature eggs). The excreta from guinea pigs with coccidiosis are loose, and can be dark colored with blood in it. The guinea pig will be obviously ill, and sit in a corner with its hair standing on end. Rapid dehydration causes loss of weight. The infection spreads via the excreta. A vet can test for the disease by having a sample of the stools analyzed.

A guinea pig with mange

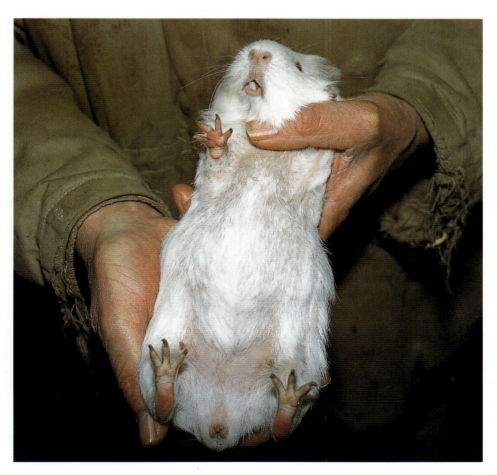

Coccidiosis is easily treated, but is best prevented by a strict hygiene regime. A hutch where the infection has occurred has to be thoroughly cleaned and disinfected, but can then still not be used for a further two weeks. The hutch, feeding bowl, and drinking bottle must of course be kept clean. If you suspect your guinea pig has coccidiosis, treat it with drugs as soon as possible.

Diarrhea

Bottom incisors that have not worn down prevent an animal feeding. Clipping the teeth is only a temporary solution.

Diarrhea can have a number of causes. With temporary diarrhea, the cause is usually a faulty diet such as too much of one food, too much green fodder, or a sudden change in diet. In such cases, feed the guinea pig on just hay and water for four days and things will usually improve. Afterward, allow the guinea pig to adapt slowly to the original diet. Diarrhea can also be a symptom of certain illnesses. If your guinea pig continues to suffer from diarrhea without appearing to be ill in other ways, a diarrhea remedy may help.

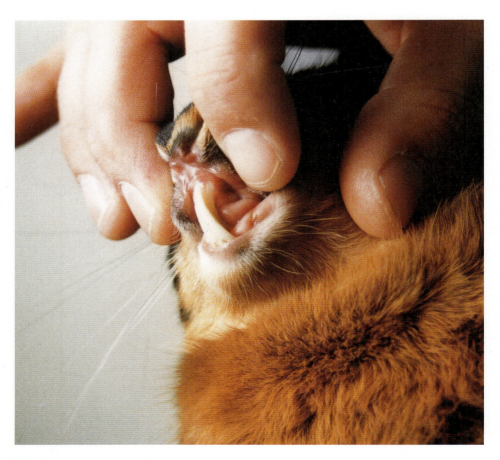

Wind

Excessive wind can occur in the gastrointestinal tract as a result of bacteria, or too much of one foodstuff, such as clover, fresh protein-rich spring hay, and some types of cabbage. Guinea pigs can overeat these foods, leading to rapid development of wind, which enlarges the belly, causes pain, and makes both it and the intestines very tense. The guinea pig can sometimes become very distressed as a result and in serious cases can die.

Wind is often treated with a household remedy but a quick visit to the veterinarian can be life- saving. While the guinea pig is recovering, avoid any green fodder for a few days, but instead feed it with easily digested food and hay. Allow the guinea pig to acclimatize itself slowly back to its normal diet.

The right diet is good for your guinea pig's health

Leukemia

Leukemia can occur in guinea pigs. The lymph nodes become enlarged, with the animal losing weight and condition while eating normally.

The presence of too many white blood cells can be determined by a blood test. The disease is not treatable.

Lice

Guinea pigs can suffer from various types of lice, but Gliricola porcelli is the commonest form. These lice are fairly thin, about 0.05 in. (1mm) long, yellow, and worm-like. These lice do not suck blood and cause so little irritation that the animals do not scratch themselves. Lice are best treated with lice powder used for cats.

Cream English Crested

Satin Coated Abyssinian guinea pig

Bicolored Peruvian guinea pig

Mites
See mange.

Canker
When buying a guinea pig, make sure the ears are clean. Although canker is more common in rabbits than guinea pigs, it is worth being alert for it. Canker is caused my ear mites. Infected animals regularly shake their heads and scratch their ears. If you push the ear lobe back slightly, you will see yellowish-brown scabs on the affected areas. Before treating with canker ointment, first thoroughly clean the ears with warm water and cotton batting. Do this very carefully. The ointment is applied to the entire ear, but read the instructions carefully. The treatment usually has to be repeated. Canker is infectious for other guinea pigs.

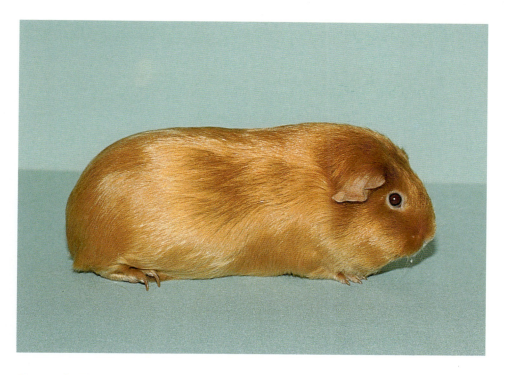

Paratyphoid

Guinea pigs that are held in close proximity with rats and mice can suffer from paratyphoid. For this reason, it is best to keep them away from rats and mice. Symptoms of paratyphoid are rapid weight loss combined with constipation and swelling of the liver and spleen. The disease takes hold rapidly and most guinea pigs will die within two to three days.

Mange (mites)

Mange causes bare patches on the skin and is caused by the Trixicarus caviae mite, which causes considerable irritation. In serious cases, a guinea pig will lose its hair together with rapid weight loss. If mange is not treated, guinea pigs can really suffer and cause themselves injury by their constant biting and scratching. The appetite is also lost in most cases. Pregnant guinea pigs are particularly susceptible to the problem, and can lose their young and even die themselves as a result. The disease can be easily recognized under a microscope and fortunately there are good remedies for mites. It is important, however, to catch the disease in its early stages.

Satin-coated Self Buff

The hair of a Rex guinea pig's coat stands on end.

Dental problems

There are two incisors and four molars in both the upper and lower jaws of a guinea pig. Rodents' teeth grow continually and also constantly wear down—provided everything goes all right. The incisors should rub against each other when eating to keep them sharp and wear them down. If the teeth are incorrectly positioned in the jaw, or the opposing tooth breaks off, the result is insufficient erosion of the incisors or none at all. In such a case, the incisor can grow into a "tusk," so that the mouth can no longer be fully closed and thus make eating impossible. The teeth can be clipped, but this is only a temporary measure and needs to be repeated every four to six weeks. The first sign that something is wrong with the teeth is when an animal slowly loses weight while still showing interest in its food. This is always a reason to check the teeth. Teeth problems can sometimes be heard. Some guinea pigs have a hereditary deformity of the jaws and these animals should never be bred. Take the trouble to make sure your guinea pig can eat properly and have the teeth trimmed if necessary, so that they do not cause wounding in the mouth. Professional help is often available for dealing with your guinea pig's teeth. Problems with the molars are more difficult to deal with. If a guinea pig suffers vitamin C deficiency, the animal will become listless and its teeth will turn yellow, loosen, and perhaps fall out.

Tumors
True tumors are fortunately not common in guinea pigs and then usually only in older animals. Only a small percentage of tumors are visible to the eye. Most are located within the body and respiratory system. Lumps on the skin are frequently not tumors, but blocked sebaceous glands or abscesses that might need treatment by a vet. A vet can suggest whether a real tumor can or should be treated.

Colds
Guinea pigs rarely suffer from colds, but can get bronchial infections that always need treatment by a vet. The infections can sometimes be cured simply with a drug.

Vitamin deficiency
(See Chapter 4.)

Worms
Guinea pigs that graze, or eat food gathered from nature, run a small risk of becoming infested with worms. These are not always visible in the droppings. Signs of worm infestation are slimy droppings and a dull and rather sparse coat. If in doubt, check with a vet. The problem can usually be cured with worm treatment.

13 SHOWING

Guinea pigs are primarily kept, by both children and adults, because they are such pleasing creatures. Some people have a preference for a particular breed, variety, or color. There is plenty of choice in these matters, as the reader will see from the chapter on breeds.

Right: A Himalayan guinea pig always has pink eyes.

Some enthusiasts belong to a club or society and take part with their animals in shows. These are extremely popular and can be held at local, state, and national levels. These shows are often combined shows with other rodents, rabbits, poultry, cage birds, and waterfowl.

Self Cream with satin coat

Such shows may often be announced as "Fur and Feather" or other misleading terms because of the wide range of animals to be shown. Shows are usually held in each area, often in the fall and winter.

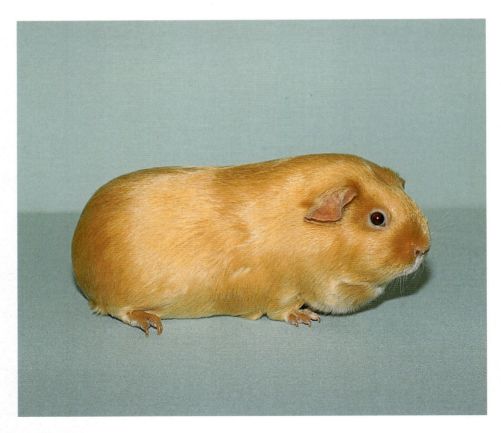

Rex-coated Golden Agouti

It may be necessary to be a member of the local or state clubs or societies to be able to enter these shows, but membership fees are usually very reasonable. A guinea pig needs to meet the breed standard in order to be shown, and there may be other conditions. A guinea pig that does not come up to standard will be disqualified by the judge.

Shows are sociable occasions in which breeders and enthusiasts compete with each other in a friendly atmosphere to see who has the finest specimens. Club shows that are not championship shows can be particularly enjoyable, but there is much that can be learned at the higher-level shows. After all there may be up to 30 or 40 breeders present and more than 200 guinea pigs on show. Competitors will have brought their best animals in the hope of winning, or at least being placed.

Some breeders only go to shows to compete, while others like to exchange ideas and information with others about breeding, care, caging, breed characteristics, and cross-breeding possibilities that might help to improve the breed. There may also be breeders who are developing a new variety or breed that they want to test before judges. In order to be eligible for a prize, the breed or variety must be recognized and meet the breed criteria. Many breeders only show their animals once each year at most because they get so much pleasure from looking after their guinea pigs at home, especially in the spring when the young are born. These breeders see a show as an enjoyable get-together with like-minded people and have less concern about winning a prize.

If you join a guinea pig club, you will be kept informed about shows and provided with details about the types of animal that may be entered. Information about shows will also include entry forms that have to be completed and returned to the show or club officials before the closing date if you wish to enter. On the day of the show, you take your guinea pig or guinea pigs to the show where they will be housed in special showing cages.

Your animal is usually then taken care of by the organization running the show. The judge will assess each specimen's build, profile, teeth, ears, eyes, stance, color of the claws, base color, and color markings, and type of coat against the breed standard. The judge's card will clearly mark each animal's strong and weak points.

Your guinea pig must be healthy, fit and clean, and have firm flesh. Pregnant guinea pigs will be disqualified from competition.

Your guinea pig should be shampooed, groomed, and its nails should be clipped. Long-haired guineas can have their hair done up in a style of your choosing. Be creative. Your guinea pig will be categorized according to its breed, color, age grouping and sex. You must decide whether your guinea pig is smooth-coated, rough-coated or long-haired. Whether you are a juvenile exhibitor or not will often be taken into consideration.

Finally, your guinea pig's demeanor is an essential aspect. Guinea pigs can be trained from an early age to keep still when being held. The friendliness of a guinea pig is much appreciated.

14 FINALLY

Your guinea pig is entirely in your care. If you take on a guinea pig as a pet, then you must also accept the responsibilities this entails. The most important of these is, of course, to keep your guinea pig happy. If you now want to find out far more about guinea pigs, then this book's objective has been achieved. Guinea pigs make such fine pets that it is well worth providing them with the right accommodation, feeding, and care that they require. If you want to know more, then contact the American Cavy Breeders Association.

Important addresses

USA and Canada
www.acbaonline.com

Guinea Pigs Online
www.guineapigs-online.com

ACKNOWLEDGEMENTS

Anatomy of the Guinea Pig, Cooper and Schiller, Harvard University Press
Diseases of Domestic Guinea Pigs, V. C. G. Richardson, Blackwell Science, Inc.
One Guinea Pig is not Enough, K. Duke, Puffin
Proper Care of Guinea Pigs, Peter Gurney, TFH Publications

The author thanks the following individuals, companies, and organizations for providing illustrations used in this book:

Aljo BV, Aviculture magazine, R. v.d. Assem, Rob Dolaard, Ferplast Benelux BV, the Goedhart family, Dr. Ilse Hamel, Willem Hoekstra, Y. Hoekstra, Stichting De Hoenderhorst, A. Kwakernaak, Gaby Prust, G. Scholtes, Theo v.d. Vliet, J. Qualm, D. Zwaan.

They each made an important contribution to this book.

The publishers wish to acknowledge the help of Mrs. Evelyne van Vliet of the National Cavy Club of the UK and Mrs. Betty Crick of the Midland Cavy Club for their help in the compilation of the English-language version of this book.